Fossils

poems by

Kindra M. McDonald

Finishing Line Press
Georgetown, Kentucky

Fossils

ACKNOWLEDGMENTS

Thank you to the following journals and their editors in which these poems
first appeared:

Alternating Currents—Warming up in the Museum of Surgical Science,
        Grinders Stand, Lost Language
New Southerner—Orbital Motion
Pure Slush—Make a Wish
Typishly—Everything Old is New Again
The Rise up Review—Deconstructing the Wall
Shot Glass Journal—Sliding
Plainsongs—Silhouette
Twyckenham Notes—The Sound of Freedom

Warming up in the Museum of Surgical Science appeared in the anthology
Spectral Lines: Poems about Scientists by Alternating Currents

Cross Country appeared in a slightly different form in the *New Fraktur Arts
Journal* under the title Keywest to Deadhorse

Publisher: Leah Maines
Editor: Christen Kincaid
Cover Art and Design: Adam Greene
Author Photo: Heidi Peelen

Printed in the USA on acid-free paper.
Order online: www.finishinglinepress.com
        also available on amazon.com

Author inquiries and mail orders:
Finishing Line Press
P. O. Box 1626
Georgetown, Kentucky 40324
U. S. A.

Table of Contents

"After that it got colder
And the world got quiet
It was never quite day or quite night
And the sea turned the color of sky
Turned the color of sea
Turned the color of ice"

—*Josh Ritter*

When We Were Careful
for Adam

You never got over the loss of your GI Joe action figure's left flipper. Wetsuit was wild and unruly, the point man of your squad and simply the best at what he did. What kind of SEAL has one flipper? Rescues were never the same again.

I always mourned the disappearance of Strawberry Shortcake's cat. That day I retraced my steps a dozen times—bedroom to deck, deck to driveway, driveway to kitchen. Custard was gone by lunch. Loyal sidekick, so even-tempered and so playful, who could know such a cat again?

You found a $100 bill in the swimming pool when you were 8. It was literally floating in front of your starfish hands and you clutched it in your fist, folded it into a tight square, secured it under the liner of your tennis shoe where it stayed all summer. Never had you felt so rich.

I found a marble that was charmed; it held every green of my future daughter's eyes. It swirled and sparked in the sunlight. It was always cool in my palm and I took it from the playground when it was flicked out of bounds by the boy who pulled my hair. I swept it into the pocket of my jean skirt, and its weight was a wish.

You lost the magic wand that came with your kit and you never understood how it vanished. You hadn't read past chapter two on tricks. There had been plans for righting wrongs with the flick of a wrist and the words on the tip of your tongue. The loss left you as empty as that hole in the magician's hat.

I lost a miniature glass Coca-Cola bottle that mysteriously drained itself when tilted upside down. I had stolen it from a neighbor's dollhouse while she was counting off the numbers in a game of hide and seek. I still don't know how it worked and thinking of it now, I wonder if I've ever felt such guilt.

You went to Greece as a child, climbed the hill of the Parthenon and carried away a chunk of ancient marble –no one had seen you, quiet as you were, kneel to tie your laces and scoop the stone into the cuff of your pant. You kept it on your nightstand near your dreams and gave it to a girl you liked years later. You miss it now.

I found an aquamarine ring in the sand under Harrison's Fishing Pier on my 15th birthday that fit perfectly. I slipped it on like it was always mine and walked away. I gave it to a boy when he went to college, who wore it on a chain near his heart, I never saw it again.

Warming Up in the Museum of Surgical Science

After the rain soaked wind off Lake Michigan
blew us in, we read about the miracle of x-rays.
Our insides reveal another medical mystery
in the shadowy folds of our stomachs.
I watch our reflections in the darkened windows
as we pass, see my heart beat faster as you hold my hand.
The light and dark of our craniums glow like halos.

This magic was catching, a technology for the masses.
The Buster Brown shoe size indicators,
the little phalanges pointing forward, a souvenir of your child's
growing foot, radiating confidence so shoes wouldn't
be outgrown by summer's end. Line your little ones up.

With his wife's hand, long-boned with thick joints,
Rontgen presented her photo to the world
and in that first x-ray she had seen her death,
the future of her rotting grave.

Now I see your back and my hip, your leg
and our ghostly teeth smiling at each other.
Our fingers overlap as you lead me outside.
Geiger counters beep as we pass, all those cell
phones pressed to bent heads, luminous.

Penmanship

Spencer replaced by Palmer
replaced by Manuscript
replaced by typewriter, keyboard,
I-pad screen.

The proper strokes, the even discipline
could reform delinquents. Writing was a path
to righteousness, to growth. Capital letters curled
side by side with lower case letters on double lined
notebooks, and always *The quick brown fox jumps over
the lazy dog.*

This is the language of love letters, this spiraling
precision. The fairy tale tongue of passed notes,
folded hearts and secret plans. Now love is late night
texts banged out over numbers and emoticons.

There is no penmanship in third grade
classrooms, no cursive on precisely angled paper
letters looping loose and indecipherable, now a secret
code, signatures are sacred, x marks the spot.
Declarations under glass
go unread.

An Homage to the Postman

Who else will mourn the notices slipped through
slots shaped like lips? They ripped the blue box
from its corner spot on Fifth street, leaving concrete
chunks to trip over, scraps of faded pick up times
trailing in the wind. I listen closer to the click
of the apartment door, the jiggle
of keys, the tricky juggle of bag and boxes.

How I will miss setting my clock to his steps on Saturdays
spent clipping coupons and wishing for a love licked
envelope one last time before the gig is gone
the snail a relic.

Headlines

Across oceans children learn writing with a brush
in the deepest India ink; letters flow like unbraided hair
smooth as a caress. Words like birds mid-flight
soar on air or swim like fish flitting between predators.
Sentences float over pages as if they could sprout wings,
grow legs, fly or sprint away.

Paragraphs are art. There is passion from setting words
on paper. How beautiful the name of God looks;
how *poetry* in characters is *word temple*
how *bombs* has such a lovely curve, drawn
like the arc of a wing or a halo.

Here we learn with upright pencils. Letters lined
up like soldiers. Small clumsy fingers curled
at awkward angles to make straight lines, consonants
at 90 degrees, vowels salute each other as they file
across the page. Even *love* looks harsh this way.

Whether we read our news left to right, down
in columns, cover-to-cover, our tears all smear
newsprint a muddled grey over words
that don't make sense. Even repeated over
and over, they feel like an extra letter
of the alphabet, thick and foreign in the mouth.
In Arabic all words look beautiful, in Urdu
there's softness in every curse, in Mandarin
and Hindi slurs are pictures—
a sweetness
that softens all words like a song
of holy or war or
holy or war or holy
or war.

The Letter Writes to the Telephone, Spring 1905

Dear Madam,

Forgive this breach
I am being bold, I admit lacking
in lady friends with whom
to correspond. As your popularity
grows, I feel compelled

Some say you'll be the death
of me, that no one
will pick up ink and paper
I must say you frighten
me. Truly, I fear obscurity.
Though I offer time and thought
and care. What you can't imagine

with your wires, your clunky crank
and dial is the tenderness
of written words, what paper holds
each perfectly crafted word. Just
the right turn
to your love, a mother, the child
you'll never hold. Intact, long after
the writer is ash.

I am intimacy and anonymity, press
me close, smeared ink, smudged
corner, a fallen tear, how close
the wrist hovered above, blood
pulsing in time with the words, racing
as my heart is now. How do you
measure love over airwaves?

You may brag at speed and reach
I traveled on horseback, on ships in
breast pockets of soldiers, in pinafores
of maidens, heart-close I am

carried, always light shining
off the mirrored surface of a still lake.

I won't be cross if you don't write.

Yours most sincerely,
Letter

The Telephone Responds to the Letter, Summer 1905

Dear Sir,

I too know the value in words.
Do not think me so callous
that I can not feel your sting,
listen close, I have wiles you can not dream.
This is not sorcery, this is evolution.
I am not tin cans and laces. Do you know
the very smallest bones of the body
reside in the ear, curled like a snail?
A miraculous design, the malleus,
the incus, the stapes—hammer, anvil
horseshoe, all listening, tingling
with the sound of another voice—
this is intimacy.
When one uses me, it is instant.
Ask via post, and wait endlessly
for an answer. How long have you
been waiting? I know those days grew
long with your regret. Did you agonize,
fear your brazen contact, and wonder if I steamed?

My dear Letter, I am flattered at your ire
you are not the first to doubt me, I have been called
instrument of the devil. How magical are sounds that live
in a thin wire. Spirits, witchcraft, touch me
during a storm and feel the shock.
This power can be consuming, Godlike how I carry
voices over air like thunder, but let me tell you Letter,
how warm it is to hear a voice you miss. I will confess
I imagine what you sound like. Would I just hear your breath,
every pause and sigh, every sharp inhale? What weight
in hesitation, every tone, in every musical laugh, the smile
of your voice can travel through me.
You see, I am the conduit, you are merely
the scribe's errand boy, an instrument
not the mystery. I am movement, connecting

coast to coast, under water, over mountains and soon
in every home. Sweet, simple letter, this is only the start
of what I can be. Are you not curious to come
to know me? Ring soon.

Yours truly and always,
Telephone

Some Advice the Sun Gave Pluto (That May Also Help You with Rejection and Poor Life Choices)

This is not your fault and you shouldn't question whether you're good enough

Dwarf planet has a nice ring to it, you're one hip asteroid and it's what's inside that counts

When one solar system closes, a black hole opens

Runts can grow up to be big and strong, it's all about believing you can do it

There are billions of stars you can hitch your wagon to, literally billions

Just because your friends do something, doesn't mean you have to follow along

Space rent just got way cheap here, think of the opportunities, not the loss

Timing is everything, who knows, in a couple dozen light years, everything could change; you have the world ahead of you, an Earth behind you

You'll look back on this and see how much you've grown, you are solid, spinning slowly in the vast dark, becoming what you were always meant to be

A Classification of the Human Race

after The Celestial Emporium of Benevolent Knowledge

a)   mirror gazers and those who practice CrossFit
b)   those that make fire and burn bridges
c)   the feral
d)   those who belong to God
e)   those who think they are gods
f)   edible
g)   the ones who when viewed through the glass of a Coke bottle
      appear as fleas
h)   ones who can rise again and again from death, the resilient ones
i)   astronauts
j)   the kind that curl into themselves like a cat grooming in a sun
      puddle
k)   those as sharp as the lines of an etch-a-sketch
l)   vegans
m)   ones who lift seashells to their ear
n)   poets

Orbital Motion

I love to sail at night
and see it
glowing on the water
the light
amongst all the darkness
how the tides
are pulled in and out
how our own
bodies are controlled
by this bright
round crater, I think of reading
to my babies,
that book *Goodnight*…in their beds how
it shone
on their pillows like liquid silver

It is what
the cow jumped over
a satellite
the shining man smiling at Earth's star
pie comes to mind,
white cheese, a full river, *Breakfast at Tiffany's*
quarter, crescent,
waning, harvest, the full on lunacy
27.3 days

on its rotation
this summer between the sun and the Earth
it will be black
I will remember somewhere in my blood
my parents hoisting
me as a newborn to the sky in that thin
ribbon of totality
the tiny pinhole glasses made from cardboard
cereal boxes
tucked behind my seashell ears and I will feel
the pull of my

axis, the water in my body, the ash and dust of my parents,
this last dark
day of my lifetime, I will tilt my face to the cooling sky, see stars
bright sharp

and I will howl.

Rising

First it was the Roman god
the messenger
deity of travelers and tricksters
swift as a rabbit
next it was the planet
the fastest moving
small and lost
in the sun's glare
then it was the element
deep in the Earth's
crust, water silver
liquid but not wet
it slithers, splits, snakes
apart and reforms as one
unit and before we knew
it was toxic
the hatters cleaned animal
pelts to make caps
the photographers captured
images as daguerreotypes
exposed the latent image
on a polished mirror
to its fumes
fixed it with salt

it is the shine on my molars
the jar in the dental office
the fever thermometers
the sharp sting of
Mercurochrome, a red-brown swipe
on my skinned knee
the maze I held, spent hours
feeding that blob through the wire
puzzle wishing to release it in my
hand to watch the quicksilver
squirm alive
it is Wednesday, water star

middle creation of the sun and the moon
a child full of woe
the shellfish in my stew
the element we just didn't know
would settle in our blood
all of us glowing silver from within

Make a Wish

I imagined the future
as an art deco Metropolis,
all shine and chrome
sleek and scalloped—

"The Jetsons" meets "The Jeffersons."
There would be teleportation,
telekinesis, pneumatic tubes for travel,
and my family would always be together.

I thought we would all be living on Mars
by now, communicating with so many
different civilizations we had all learned
Esperanto and discoveries occurred so

many times per day, there were whole
cities devoted to cataloging new species.
Flowers that changed color based
on who looked at them, fish that

competed to hold their breath the longest
on land, and the detailed study of Mars birds would
allow us to recreate flight, as we preened our feathers
and understood inherently our wild purpose

yet every year on August 5th, the Curiosity Rover sings
"Happy Birthday" to itself, the universal tune echoing
lonely through the cold dark vast.

A Funeral for the Discontinued

It is raining, as it should be.
The Thimble and the Iron hold flowers
the Boot—the very symbol of hard work
is stoic and sturdy

as the light brown m and m's make a circle
and gossip with Chipper the chipmunk
and Honks the goose, who carry
condolences from the other beanie babies

Mulberry, Raw Umber and Violet Blue
are sharp and straight as they prepare
one of their own for the next life.
Dandelion Crayon how we loved you—
just the right shade of spring you will always be
the first food for the bees after winter
and the best choice for the sun.

The pet rocks toss handfuls of dirt symbolically
everyone hums a Guns and Roses refrain
He-Man hands out autographed Polaroid's
and the Chrysler LeBaron's, their mile wide hoods
gleaming like homecoming queens, wait to drive
the gang to lunch where they will dine on Crystal
Pepsi and Ben and Jerry's Wavy Gravy—
delicacies as rare as a quick game of Monopoly

the dandelions have matured into puffs
the seeds lean into the breeze, pick a handful—
wish, and watch them soar, move on.

Everything Old is New Again

In 1990 my sixth grade class buried
a time capsule. In our photo we are armed
with hard hats that glint in the sun, shovels
in our outstretched hands, smiles bright.

We collected what we held dear and what most
represented our time on the brink of adolescence
at the edge of a new decade at the end of a century.
We wrote letters to our future selves

what we hoped for and worried about and loved—
notes scratched out in *Simpson's* spiral-bound pages
or typed and published from our class dot-matrix
printer, its rough-torn edges and bumpy paper teeth

an exercise in patience. In went a floppy disc
of *The Oregon Trail* and home movies on VHS cassettes,
there were mix tapes and Air Jordan sneakers,
headlines of Operation Desert Shield, Mandela's release

and the magic of the Hubble telescope
floating somewhere in the blackness of space,
watching us all and learning. On my list of
treasures I wrote about my library card,

how it was freedom, how I had spent that year
learning the Dewey Decimal system and sifting
through the card catalogs that smelled of toast
and mothballs. The sturdy oak, the tarnished

brass, which drawers stuck and which ones
screeched, all the many hands that slid those
long gone cards in place, faded; all those cabinets
selling for thousands now at auctions.

I wrote about my typewriter, passed down from
my dad. It weighed more than a bowling ball

and clacked and whirred and dinged my stories
to life, the Wite-Out layers thick and cracked

on my pages. I worried about the ozone, drug use,
the homeless man I saw on our park bench, all
of the fathers going off to fight in a desert, the vicious
spirit of racism, the cost of college. I hoped for love
and wrote a want-ad for my future husband, kind
and funny an explorer and a patient soul, imagining
our future unspooling like a fishing line into a sea
we would carry each other on like life rafts.

All these years later and I'm curled up with him as the news
talks of fire and fury, the new shock and awe. I've learned
never to use conditioner in the event of a nuclear blast
the fallout can slip into the crevices of a human hair trapped

by the smooth detangling properties of conditioner. In
sixth grade we practiced hallway tornado drills on knees
with ducked heads and hands over our tender necks, not
unlike my parents and their air raid exercises.

We lay together and I think of my parent's
waterbed, how all us kids floated on that cool
surface watching movies on the VCR, the cobalt
blue of the Blockbuster video cases stacked up.

Somewhere someone is still racking up
late fees, a thrift store wallet holds a movie
rental card that tell us *be kind, rewind*, oh
the dreams we would have on those waves now.

Tonight's sunset is as pink as the belly
of a salmon, no mushroom clouds billowing
in the distance, no rumbling storms, just an echo
of those lists of worries and a cracked concrete

capsule seal, reminding us some things never change.

Rule of Thumb
(a found poem)

A man may beat his wife
with a stick so long
as it is no thicker than his thumb

state law prohibits a woman
from driving a car on a main street
unless her husband
waves a red flag to alert
other drivers

women may not wear patent leather
shoes in public or adjust their stockings
a lady may not lift her skirt
more than six inches while walking
through a mud puddle

a woman's hair belongs to her spouse
and she must have his permission
before going to the stylist

women must be swathed in at least
16 yards of fabric
it is against the law to walk alone
on a train track
or to jump off a bridge

A Future Excavation of Earth

Bone-sniffing dogs
have identified the precise spot
on a remote island where Amelia

Earhart died, beneath a ren tree
waving its slender leaves
in the breeze and casting shade

patterns in the shapes of tiny
airplanes. The dogs one by
one lay down at the tree's base

alerting their trainers with locked
eyes to the scent of long decomposed
bones. The circular charcoal rings

of an 80 year old campfire steps
away, warmed her thin skin
on a cold night, the smell of home

a jackknife, her compact with
the mirror still in tact, the latch
that had to be pushed just so—

a zipper pull and glass jars
scattered around the dirt.
When we are excavated

all ash and dust, the archeologists
will play in our square boxes bobbing
on water. They will splash and sing

to the stars, hold our rectangles up
to the sky, the apple symbols reflecting
the sun. They'll laugh at our streetlights

a system of power poles, think—

why would one light up the whole night
just to see in the dark? They'll believe

our currency was plastic straws
all our books locked away in storage
no evidence of a working alphabet

only towering symbols and fading
graffiti. They'll believe we failed
to devise a system for waste disposal

living alongside our litter and our
dead and as they shake their heads
they will scoop the minerals from

our bones into soft mounds of soil
fill their sample bags and seal them,
add the label, earthling fossils.

Compound

Tired of playing pinball in The Alouette Lounge
long after the stacks of quarters were gone

sugarsick from Shirley Temples, I turned to
flipping through the payphone white pages

searching for anything to read in this smoky
neon dark, making up stories for the people

on Avondale Avenue, another father who
would harbor me, not hitchhike bar to bar.

He toasts again and again and I chew on words
remembering my lessons in compounds, aching

to find what hides in something else. In the word
bartender, a kind and loving bar, a gentleman of

mild temperament. Is raincheck wet?
Friendship sailing or sinking? Firearm painful

hot? These words fractured and repaired
together bound to reveal their secrets,

whispering to me as we leave late. Someday
I'll forgive this backslide, the foreshadowing,

moonlight on blackice, his eyes like butterscotch
apologies smell of firewater, forgotten headlights,

hairpin curve, snowbank, blackout then handcuff,
jailhouse, nightmare, goodbye fatherland.

Words swell in my head making houses
to dwell in, a separate neighborhood

carefree, peaceful, hear me now,
there is always a lie in believe.

Deconstructing the Wall - November 9th, 2009

As the news clips played out, I watched
again as brick by brick of that foreign wall
fell, and suddenly I was a child all over

and my father was urging me inside the house
to watch this, because *this is history.* Here
it was once more. I am grown and he is dying

and we had spent the last 4 months
trying to break down our own walls
learning how much work it takes

for them to fall, the wreckage, a promise
that hope can prevail. I had called him
that day, an act of penance, to see if

he remembered us together twenty
years ago. We watched the archived
footage from our separate homes

joined by phone lines, a quiet cancer.
Tears collecting in our shirt collars
as cheering people gripping rubble raised

fists to the sky, smiles glowing like pearls.
I did not know then he would live only
34 more days; that forgiveness is

letting go, smoothing souvenirs
of concrete into polished wishes.
I did not know 7 years later, my

country would chant *build the wall.*

Seen and Not Heard
(a found poem)

Who was she?
One that speaks
herself, as am I.
She thought the brain,
greatest queen,
the quiet tone—
remarks grown aged,
remarks she managed
beautifully.

She learned things, of course.
Why the belt in all ills?
Timid and smiling children
will please sulky soldiers.
They're least remarked on.
Telescopes bleed,
all their sentences shout
on white cards,
the startled anything faces.

It was the just course, they said.
She upon the table, hands out.
The agreed upon: lazy,
simple, but prettier, (exclamation added).
What's the ground? It's one world.

She learned of course,
then the time of getting snapped
in traps. She breaks beautiful
piece by little pleading
puzzled piece.

(Source text remixed—Carroll, Lewis, 1832-1898. (2000). Alice's adventures in
Wonderland. Peterborough, Ont. :Broadview Press.)

An Elegy for the Sears and Roebuck and a Grandfather I Never Knew

Clelly ran the freight elevator
at the second largest Sears in the U.S.
took up a whole city block in Louisville
ran shipping and delivery for those catalog
orders going all over the country
and while he hauled the boxes
directed the forklifts and orchestrated
the interstate of conveyer belts
his daughters sat on the kitchen
linoleum of their rural home pouring
over the catalog that had everything
unmentionable underwear
tools and tires
dog collars and dishwashers
dresses dreamed over and circled
swing set centerfolds marked by
creased corner wishes
they made entire congregations
of paper dolls from catalog covers
dressed in the latest designs cut
from glossy pages, a fashion show every night
when he came home scooped up each girl
and kissed their heads conducting a dance
between them as they bounced
from knee to foot and sometimes
their wishes would materialize in his hands
a red dress for mama—his always Ruby
a perfect pair of patent leather loafers
the teddy bear with the softest paws
all so much better than their picture
parts those gifts he carried home from
the place that buzzed electric
now shuttered still as store mannequins
a plaque that reads national register
of historic places, you just say, *my*
dad worked here, he was a good man.

Prefix

The handmade felt magnets hung
on their avocado green fridge.
One giant cow, said "Holy cow, are you eating again?"
The other magnet had two owls leaning
towards each other on a branch. One said, "I'm tired"
the other "I'm retired."

Retired. Six years old, and I read this over
and over, those endless summers taking shelter
with my grandparents, puzzling over the prefix "re"
like repeat or retry or redeem. Tired again?
Is one owl more tired than the other?
This confused me.

My grandfather who was always retired
would take me to the Yankee Doodle Donut
and talk about this small town that doesn't change
and just tires people out. When he was a schoolboy
working at bowling alleys, he set up the wooden pins
by hand. This was hot work. Sitting fearless on the ledge
as the balls hurled towards him. Working fast on a strike,
dodging the roll and ducking for 5 pins in one hand
and 5 in the other, praying for no splits, the fast scoop—
the reset, re-rack, repeat life of a pinsetter.

This town changed, though. Installed the slick under-lane
return, the metal arms that reach and rack, and the automated
pulley that lowers him gently underground.
We all feel retired, so much more tired than we were yesterday.
Pinboys dodging strikes for a nickel a lane
and no dental plan.

The felt magnets are soft in my hand, leaving
their imprint on the freezer door.

Craftsman

Yesterday the radio reported Sears is on life support—
closing even more stores, the once tower, the once
empire-department icon, joins the rubble
of brick and mortar, a little bit of America crumbles.
Ghosts make love in abandoned dressing rooms
and race lawnmowers around dark aisles.
They still remember the heyday when every want
was available there, where quality was a name—
houses could be ordered, honor built with dreams
and sweat and kits, a mail-order life of precut lumber
shipped by railroad boxcar, the 30,000 parts deposited
on land became a home and the center of America is still
dotted with them. The Craftsman floor plans call out
their names like angels on roll call: Alhambra, Avondale,
Crescent, Westley.

Today in Newport News near the shipyard, sailors
and laborers eat lunch under shade trees by the Greenlawn
cemetery, where the office is a 1936 Sears Catalog home
that keeps watch over the Confederate prisoners of war
who steal whiskey off the night guards and take turns
moving the Union headstones to face south,
children pick dandelions, and spouses still
quarrel in their graves.
The men play solitaire
the women knit hats
the house is solid, proud.

Silhouette

Portraits of my great grandparents are serious.
Who could hold a smile for the length of time
it took to record an image? Most days my cheeks hurt
from holding my smile up so high. Still we grin and pose
captured in a flash. A forgotten day until the bent-eared
square appears years later in some relative's attic album.
The Navajo and Amish refuse photos, slipping a bit
of their selves onto cells, the sacrilege of all of it.
Scoop your reflection from a pool of water,
this is your picture, the memory of it shivers.

When they were courting, young lovers
had their silhouettes crafted, cut from paper
and tucked away into lockets or pocket watches.
Tell me what you can see of your dearest in this dark
profile. Imagine the storm cloud eyes, the freckle
sprinkled nose, the soft sweet frown of mouth.
The featureless paper let the mind work magic
committing to memory every eyelash of love.

When Facebook Announces it's the Birthday of Your Friend that Died

And it becomes clear very quickly that some people
do not know that this friend is dead, that their friend
and yours is not getting these wishes for a perfect year
ahead, and to have the best day ever

but you are getting these reminders and every one
is like drinking hot lead and by the end of the day
it has pooled into a heavy weight in your gut the shape
of a bullet and it is lodged near your spleen

some are concerned that their wishes are belated and
some are profound, "treasure yesterday, celebrate today,
welcome tomorrow" and thank you for being born
which is a sentiment I agree with

and finally the friend's relatives indicate that this friend
has had an end of life experience and that this will be
the last post from their account.

What I Will Remember on the Brink of WWIII

We sat crisscross
applesauce on the
Berber carpet, rough
loops plucked by our
fingers unspooling runs
in the goldenrod thread,
itchy in my turtleneck
and sweater, radiator
spitting steam against
our Pennsylvania winter
hot and sleepy after lunch
it was Monday show and tell
and we circled one by
one fidgeting with our
treasures, presenting
them with stories we
had practiced all weekend

we all stared at Steven
with a Samsonite suitcase,
all hard corners and shiny
latches, bigger than three
of us put together
his father's travel tags
tied around the handles
we wondered what marvels
it held as he shied away each
time Ms. Miller called on him
teasing us with anticipation
every round he passed on
the reveal holding out until
we had all shared our shows
with breath held and the hands
of a magician he flicked those
latches, snapping them up
on springs and threw open
the heavy case dark as our

tornado cellar, inside the ripped
and shredded satin lining lay
six still kittens, quiet as the sheet
pulled over me when I slept—
their eyes hopscotch rocks
their paws blood raw from
hours clawing for breath.

The Letter Rejects the Telephone Outright, Autumn 1905

Madam,

Never have I been addressed in such fashion.
You surely think highly of yourself, have plenty
to say, but have you listened? Shall we debate
the difference between hearing and listening?

You speak of the beauty of sound, the link between
vocal chords and eardrum but I believe you do not listen.
I reject your claims that you will outlast me.
How immune we become to sound. In time
you will no longer hear the nightly train whistle
when it once kept you awake. I see your future
well, dear Telephone. Humans retain only fractions
of what they hear. How will you compete
with the noise of this world?

You will come to be a nuisance, a vessel
for all the spiders in the web, the switches
and operators flipping lights and plugging cords
connecting town and country, an enormous system
of gossip, rumor and bother.

Words on paper will always remain, Telephone.
You can go back again and again to it, while your sounds
just vanish through the air, a voice we will swat silent.

Most Sincerely,

Letter

The Telephone Acknowledges the Letter's Merit and Suggests a Truce, Winter 1906

Sweet Letter,

You are irresistible when you are righteous
stewing away in indignation. It tickles me
to think of you brooding.
I will admit your points have merit,
I have quite enjoyed our clandestine
correspondence and confess to have reread
a line or two from your hand. About listening
I will only say there is splendor in the noise
around us. Listen—the hammering of the beams
is a waltz: one, two, three, one, two, three—
the children playing hide and seek are a choir,
my heart is the beat of the broken carriage wheel
squeak, I urge you to listen as well, dear Letter,
do you hear me on the wind? Do you feel me on your skin.
Lest you think me difficult to teach, I will offer you this truce,
we are both worthy, maybe one day we can compliment each other.
What you fear most in your secret heart is your death
I don't believe that I could kill.
I am being prepared for my permanent home
in the postal office downtown, I do believe we will meet soon,
Letter, it is our destiny, or perhaps just gossip.

Fondly,

Telephone

Meditation

Out the sixth floor window of the yoga studio
how quickly it has become dark.

Now when I roll myself out to forget the Monday,
it is full on night as I try to keep

my mind inside this room. I see how the Christmas
lights have been strung across

the high sails of the old battle ship and buildings have
been outlined in bulbs that shine

against the shipyards and reflect on the brackish water
to make it gleam like jewels.

I breathe, try to focus on my posture when someone
lights a cigarette from the high rise

balcony six blocks away. It is so clear against all this dark
this bright flame, this small red circle

of stress relief glowing in an invisible hand. I used to love
to smoke in the winter, I see us so distinctly

I'm lightheaded as rings circle us, you cup your hand to my match
and we inhale and exhale away the day

you in your perch above the city and me on this mat in this room
where I write a poem in my head

I keep trying to clear of thoughts.

Strike

You have collected all
the matchbooks that
we never see anymore.
Like payphones, they used
to be everywhere until all
at once, they are nowhere.
A calling card for every service
every bar and business
had a stash; hotels and bail
bonds, country clubs and call
girls, car dealers, insurance sales
and wedding favors – *Mary
and Tom, forever,* light your
cigarettes.

You gathered them all
in glass containers that sit
nested together in front of
our fireplace, a hazard—
all those tips of phosphorus
comfortably cuddled with chlorate,
this is our level of risk these days.
All the decades pressing into each
other, matches passed to you from
family, lost friends, pen-pal soldiers.
Some showy gold leaf and italics all
gloss and polish, others bare and stark
obvious, *Matches,* they yell in bold black.
There are Vegas showgirls who shimmy
with a flick of the cover,
fish that swim and shimmer
in embossed metallic foil,
samurai swords and sports cars,
many variations on the female form.

Sometimes I sneak into
the piles reach deep and hope

to retrieve one I've never
seen before; these are good
days, a reminder that
surprises still exist. All
these books waiting to
combust, curated like a history
exhibit, are a sign that somewhere
else their siblings live in
the back pocket of a pair
of unwashed Levi's,
between loveseat cushions,
propping up the uneven
table legs at so many restaurants,
and in junked glove compartments—
they still ignite birthday candles,
lanterns in a power outage,
pilot lights and campfires.

The rough cat tongue scratch
of the tip across that strip,
the struck surface all friction
and heat, the snap of the stick,
the curl of the flame and the
cool autumn nights when I still
want to strike the match to
hear the flare, smell the sulfur,
this remains.

Grinder's Stand

You squint in the firelight sketching
out the new world
a canvas of chance.
You, greatest pathfinder,
quiet explorer by starlight.
You and your new brother, now
forever conjoined to your name;
a Siamese twin in history
with his few months study of astronomy
and map making.

The quiet would build such pressure
upon the ears there was music in it.
Such open space all around, land and horizon,
just sky and the possibility of beyond. Winding
with the Snake and Salmon rivers you discover
what you were born to do.

After this, how could you sit down
to business, to govern? When always
there's the wider earth, the dark spaces
to uncover. And now so much noise, so much
chatter and everything so small—
all paths already forged,
each wall closing in.
Coyotes in the shadows
howling from the corners.

Lewis, just you, alone pacing
the wood floors of a rented room.
Is it the land that's calling you?
Is it that great ocean and what's beyond?
Or the scotch and the opium that dull your senses?
That moonless night how your hand shook
with the weight of the gun leaving
you cold in morning. You, now a memorial
lurking on an ancient trail

with every stone explored,
every patch of dirt memorized.

Sepia

In the photo
my grandfather kept
the limbs
are piled up
neatly like firewood
a row of legs straight as soldiers
arms all crossed
a boy in uniform
on a stretcher
bandaged stumps
and just off frame
the surgeon
sawing

The Sound of Freedom

My neighbor wakes up screaming most nights.
I wouldn't hear him if I spent my nights asleep
and not outside trying to make sense
of the stars and tracing constellations

to find a cure for insomnia.
His wife must soothe him back to sleep
with her warm breath, her skin that smells
like lavender, her whispers that the bed is

soft and solid, not a moving tank in a shaken
snowglobe of sand.
When he was deployed I heard her on the patio
throwing dishes, crash after satisfying crash

of cheap wedding shower china the cymbal
ring of loneliness. Later she would tell me
they taught her that in wife school
take your anger and a Sharpie, write out

the harbored hurt on plates and cups
the bottled words like hate and hard and fuck
and hurl it onto concrete, splintered shards
of rage until it is all powder and dust.

After the fireworks lit the sky, all the illegal
rockets shot by drunk boys playing war
the whistles and pops echoing through our suburb
the bang like bursting soup bowls.

The cats cower in the hall away from windows,
the dog is under the bed whimpering.
My neighbor is on his belly taking cover
seeing his friend in pieces over and over.

Walking through my backyard my feet are slick
with mulberry juice. In the morning, smoke will

linger thick on the air, seep through the windows,
I will see footprints on my carpet, dark as blood.

It Begins (or How a Suicide Bomber is like a Dancing Bear)

When he takes their photos, lines them
up and loads the film.
They are shy in their fierceness and so young.
Their minds shaped, their spirits molded.
What they come to know is this is right.
This is just. This is how they walk and what they carry.
This is the purpose of their days.

How it begins is slow and repetitive.
He plays a jaunty tune on the rebec
Heats the plate with coals shoveled from the brazier.
They are lined up taken young from their mothers.
Had their claws ripped out and their mouths
muzzled. Harnessed and leashed they are
forever instruments.

Their photo is like a resume when they die
fighting for obligation or a promise of heaven.
Eyes glinting like the sun off the weapon that their hands have
grown to fit now like another limb or the weight of an infant
son they'll never bear.
Glory to god with a gun.

On the searing metal hopping from paw to
paw the music is the torture and it commences.
How they learn to dance this agony, the blisters
searing the soles, charring the hair, performing
for the fear of standing still.

Their martyr pictures hang on family walls, in their pockets they carry
photos of their mothers. He watches them leave knowing their next
mission may be a chest heavy with C4. They go forward
staging their lessons. The words are music in their heads
as someone's plan is executed.

He plays the music faster for the crowd that's
gathered. Coins tossed in the tin clang fear

into labored bodies stepping faster.
Bent and scared, scarred and tamed
forgetting how it once was to be wild.

Hear the music and perform to death.
See the enemy and become small photos of mothers
littering the street like confetti. The promise was
only a hole in the ground covered with dirt.

Cross Country

Today in Alaska the sun set
at 1:25 PM and will not
rise for two months.

On your journey from Key West
to Deadhorse with nothing
but rage and the 64 points
of the Google directions
you've memorized. Between
skin slick with suntan oil
and an oil-field town not found
on the map are 1,169 miles
of ghosts and lonesome roads
that are seasonally closed. Still
you start in autumn, trying to outrun
a war, you begin the combat

where you're caught in a lightning storm
outside Saskatchewan,
where you're caught in a blizzard
near Bismark. You wait, folding
atlas pages into perfect origami
swans, tear your maps
into paper airplanes
and send them soaring
out the window, flying
above your car on the solitary
stretch of hypnotizing highway.

Your invisible passengers make paper dolls
from coffee shop napkins and stick figures
on the hot breath fog of the rearview mirror
guiding you along with their quiet navigation,
their contrition, their forgiveness.

The sun returns, you learn to sleep again.

After Months on the Couch Where You Wore a Hole Through Your Oversized Sweater

You heard the wood thrush sing for the first time
this year, his flute song carried you outside
yourself to a spring you didn't know was beyond the living
room. In the crying months, the child next door
had learned to balance without training wheels.

People still blew out candles and licked frosting from their ends.
There were first long, slow kisses, rice was thrown,
children learned to write their names and paddle
to the deep end of the pool. All despite your daughter found
clutching a bottle of pills, despite your own wicked fall into chemo hell.

Life persisted, like the robin you found naked and limp,
fed by an eye dropper, taught to bathe on its own—

and released from your cupped hands,
arms and eyes raised
to the pine in prayer.

Some Tips on Being Yourself

Anyone can be a hostess.
See how much you can class up your act.
Sometimes I take the eviction notice off
my door. Sprinkle a trail of glitter,
imagine a fairy had come to visit.
It should appear as though
you've used witchcraft.

I love aprons I feel naked without one.
I like to prepare a meal that doesn't require
knives. My mother got this recipe out of *Playboy*.
Keep the cocktails flowing,
have sing-alongs, some melodrama,
use pirate imagery.
Don't confuse pick-pocketing
as an ice breaker.

Try this for introductions:
this is Sue, she can't have children,
John's on mood stabilizers,
Benny just got fired.

I find I can judge people
by the temperature of their steak.
When not fed quickly
they can become confused and easily
agitated like a bear fresh from hibernation
light fuse and back away
never look one in the eye
until the forest beckons.

Listen when they talk about the past.

I have chosen paint colors based
on their names alone,
            too drunk to hail a cab.

Like a lightning bolt,
sometimes you're the cause
of your own mishap.

Defining

When the Earth was flat and square
the four corners pointed out at nothing
the stars unraveled like stitches
and the world stopped at the jagged

edges like a torn page. There were
boundaries, the safety of guardrails
of confines and finish lines, a creation
stretched as tight as a canvas and us

a watercolor painted point at the sweet
center. Then someone ventured towards
the edge and found no exclamation mark,
just an infinite series of ellipses that circled

and circled back. Lines were drawn and re-drawn,
stars were charted and our domain grew so large
we vanished. Maps rolled out in captain's quarters
on a roiling sea, or on a king's table far from the front

splotched with gravy, sketched with sirens, a grand
rough approximation of a world as we knew it.
From sextants to software, we carry maps in our
pockets, we zoom over and into, walk through

this great frontier. Is our world bigger or smaller?
From space I can see our continent, country, state,
city, street, home, bed, you and I hands clasped
together, still at the center of it all, spinning.

A Mineral Element

In this notebook I found
two hangman games from
a plane trip. "Possum" won
with a head, body and left arm.
"Bauxite" hung with a full body, including
eyes, nose and a frown. I have never used
bauxite in a poem.
Also, a half written restaurant review
praising the creaminess of the grits,
an email address and phone number with
no name. I consider dialing and decide better.
A draft of the speech I'll later read at my father's
funeral from note cards. A license plate number
of a reckless driver. A book title, and now this poem
that I'll lose and find again, and remember writing
at a corner table by a crossword player tapping his pen
to the music, and a couple in matching coral shirts that
darken my sunny mood as they say "malignant" three times.

…Makes you Stronger

The Buick at the intersection of Little Creek and Waters

a bottle of Cachaca after a handful of Excedrin PM

the rotted gallbladder

that night that guy you didn't really know, drove you somehow back to
your hotel room after you matched each other shot for shot on Alabama
Slammers, the details are fuzzy

the rope swing in the Dismal Swamp Canal

x-ray after x-ray after x-ray

the hazelnuts

that one time with whip-its

Aspartame

a blood sugar spike

that fall when your high heel caught in the cuff of your pants and you
blacked out at the bottom of the stairs, your hair didn't grow in the soft spot
on your head for a year

whatever exists in the cheese in Tijuana

a tick you picked up hiking the York River trail

the fibrous tissue slowly forming in the lining of a chest, the abdominal
cavity, the scarring of the lungs from the very air he breathed, the clothes
we washed, the work they were paid to do—

what doesn't kill, makes it mark, catches up with you.

Sliding

Last week you lost your pearls
and claimed a conspiracy.
Tuesday the book you assured the library you returned
was found like teeth under your pillow.
Tonight you'll look at your wedding portrait
say, *Who is that lovely girl?*
Tomorrow you will lose my name.

Amazon Answers a Few of Life's Questions

Will this fan work in the dark?
>If you're scared of the dark, find the light.

Can this fan blend pancake batter?
>It can blend batter, but it's better if you have a partner.

If I set my worries down in front of this fan, will it blow them all away?
>It depends on how heavy your worries are. If they are less than the weight
of the sun in grams, then yes.

Will this watch make up for lost time?
>As far as the indefinite continued progress of existence, no. Your breaths
occur in irreversible succession from the past through the present.

How does this watch measure time?
>By the sun, the moon and the stars. By the change in the shadow's
direction, by the lines forming on your face.

If I am drowning, will the watch know?
>As you take in water, your oxygen supply will slow, your body will relax,
your lungs will fill with water, beautiful buoyant balloons, you will sink,
time will go on.

Is the cake a lie?
>No, it is moist and delicious, you should always eat cake.

Lost Language

"Some endangered languages, are being revived by young people and through poetry."
—*United Nations Educational, Scientific and Cultural Organization*

Shorter now than the lifespan of a mayfly
these words do not even mate.

Nothing left to paint a blue streak as language
dies before an alphabet is written.

The fragments left hanging in the air
fall silent as each native expires.

When all the speakers get together there is no
one to talk to. The word "we" has disappeared.

Walk past the language graveyards, breath
held for miles. Culture's tongue bitten

as words turn to ash in our mouth.
Rake charcoal from your dry lips

how they burned me with their heat.
Lick your mother tongue, find relief

in your little ones, poets sing this water, praise
this balm. It is here separating us, drink.

End of Life Haiku

Earth keeps on turning
outside my window, ashamed
of my stubborn ways

My teeth in a glass
sit on the bedside table
trying to speak out

Old photo smiles
pretty girl stares, who is she?
that was me, I think.

A face I don't know
frame smashed into jagged shards
beauty long faded

Each day passes slow
after a lifetime flies by
body suspends mind

Mind sifts memories
like flour just leaving dust
to gather on me

My words make no sense
thoughts as fractured as cobwebs
sounds underwater

Voices linger still
parts of songs, muted colors
fades faster each day

Mirror reflection
each glance as shooting as pain
where am I in there?

My New American Dream

> *"If you are curious, capable and resourceful with a deep sense of*
> *purpose, then you can go to Mars."*
> —Dying in Space: An American Dream, The Atlantic, April 2013

If all goes according to plan, I will depart
Earth in 2023. I will not be coming back.
I will bring a good book.

It's obviously quite dangerous if something
unforeseen went wrong of course, human attention
being what it is, but I have dreamt of dying on Mars

(just not on impact). I am ready to fly
I'm not alone in that. I think of my grandfather
who came from Scotland to America, took a rickety

boat across the sea, and went west
into wilderness. Did he stop
because of the risks?

I've spent my life, if it ends in space,
that's not a bad way to go.

Collision

In the office kitchen this morning, an ant hefts a crumb,
of a Pop-Tart edge twice the size of his body and marches
it across the counter. It is miles to the window, days to the door.
When I intercept it on the edge of the counter, I remember
that the Chinese space station is due to fall to earth this week
sometime between Monday and Wednesday give or take 16 hours
somewhere between Nebraska and Tasmania give or take the Pacific
Ocean and pulled by atmospheric drag it will hurtle towards earth
at the rate of 1,000 kilometers, ripping off its exterior parts.

I read that the chance of being hit by space debris is extremely low,
in fact, the odds of a Powerball jackpot are higher and since it has
been so long since I have played the lottery, about as long as it has
been since I have been drunk, I decide to coax the ant onto
the tip of my index finger. Carry it down 7 floors to the street
where I pretend it is not stepped on by the thousands of feet
that pass this very place every day.

Luray Caverns After a Fight

Like the stillness of a crane
the cavern calms us
how everything is quiet
how our pulse slows
and our chests open
and we can breathe deeper.
Here, it is tranquil
cooling our hot heads
we see more clearly in the dark
than we could up above.

I think of the men, who decades before
explored the trickling sounds beneath their feet
tracked the cold coming from the summer ground
and decided to dig.
Ever so slowly peeling back the earth
lighting their way with flames
into the dark void, and gasping at the world below.

I forget now why I was angry.
My heart feels cavernous
like love could be mirrored in the
reflection of the collected waters
of years of slow and steady dripping.
A love I believe in like the promise
of the splash of a wish
at the bottom of a well.

Melting

We are apart on either side of falling
snow. The world now layered blankets
thick as buttercream, our hearts race
to each other across telephone lines
since our bodies are still separated
by the distance of a city's single snowplow
and our rear-wheel drive cars.
We are on the brink of moving
forward or stalling in this blizzard.
I make tunnels for you to crawl through
but you're claustrophobic and have become crazy
bored by your mirror reflection
you describe your now bare face to me, shaved
for the first time in a decade.
Imagine my lips being first to touch that dip
between your lips and chin.

After days of negotiations by phone, we thaw,
commit to this life, a union solid
and frightening as ice.
Finally we meet across snow banks, you are raw
and wind struck, I am weathered, but warmer. Shy
as strangers, we reveal, uncover, then cling and hibernate
until it is unclear where we end and angels begin
the snowman watches us heat each other
from the inside out. Stubble returns slow to your face
covers our promises sealing them like a psalm on the tips
of our tongues.

Six Ways to Start a Fire Without a Match

First we pretend it is a matter of survival.
We are not in our backyard using sticks
that have been kept dry in the garage.
Innately we have learned how to distinguish
softwoods from a distance and gathered
willow, aspen, juniper.

I
Friction-based fire making:
A spark will form at 800 degrees.
We sit cross legged under the pine that has grown tired of its needles
and made a bed for us, and the perfect tinder. It seems important to be quiet.
You hold, I spin; you spin, I hold. We will need to build shelter.
We spin and spin, I try to wish the heat in my hands into the kindling.
My eyes wander to the bucket of water you prepared earlier
and set aside in case our conflagration can't be contained.
I am buoyed by your confidence.
The water was gathered from a distant stream, carried carefully—
it could be what sustains us.

II
Two-man friction drill:
One person applies downward pressure, the other rapidly spins the string.
We remember, we do in fact have string. I make a solo trek for it and scissors.
 I leave the lighter, hurry back to your side. We are losing light.
A walnut shell anchors the stick, but keeps cracking. The string has frayed
as thin as threads of hair. Does the spider know how beautiful her web looks at
dusk?

III
Fire plough:
Pushing out particles of wood ahead of the friction will ignite the tinder.
You cut a groove in a fireboard with the knife on your keychain. Such silly things—
keys in a place like this. There are at least seven shades of green in the forest and
when I can find a small square of sky through the green, it is the very color of
your eyes. A pile of wood shavings builds, but nothing ignites. How many hours
is 800 degrees?

IV
Pump Fire drill
Invented by the Iroquois using a fly wheel to generate friction.
We need a flywheel, a spindle, fireboard, cross bar,
a leather strap. We do not have four of these.
It is easy to believe we are the only people who remain.

V
Bow drill:
The drill must be hard or slightly harder than the fireboard.
Catch the drill in a loop of the bowstring; then vigorously saw back and forth.
We have become efficient at maintaining speed and pressure. Do you hear
the music of fire? It is a whisper. It is your breath on my neck. The wood is singing
of cold. We tilt our heads in unison as the sweat runs off our noses.
The slightest drop could stifle any spark.

VI
Spark-based fire making with flint and rock:
How you care for the spark will determine your survival.
The type of rock is important. Quartzite is best and can be identified
by crescent shaped fractures; these form when the moon consoles the rock.
We have long abandoned our shoes, so that our feet can feel
the paths, we are becoming what we were meant to be. I can hear the deer before
I can see it. What is the name of spark? Could we call it with our striking?
This is our language now.

Kindra **McDonald** received her MFA from Queens University of Charlotte. She teaches poetry at The Muse Writers Center and is an adjunct writing professor and sometimes doctoral student. Her work has appeared in various journals and anthologies. She is the author of the chapbooks *Concealed Weapons* and *Elements and Briars* and the poetry collections *Fossils* and *In the Meat Years*, (forthcoming). She has been nominated for a Pushcart Prize and for Bettering American Poetry. She lives in the city of mermaids with her husband and cats and she changes hobbies monthly.

http://www.kindramcdonald.com/

www.ingramcontent.com/pod-product-compliance
Lightning Source LLC
Chambersburg PA
CBHW021201090426
42740CB00008B/1188